The Peace Corps is a U.S. government agency. Since its launch in 1961, the Peace Corps has aimed to promote world peace and friendship by:

- *Helping the people of interested countries in meeting their need for trained men and women.*

- *Helping promote a better understanding of Americans on the part of the peoples served.*

- *Helping promote a better understanding of other peoples on the part of Americans.*

Over 200,000 Volunteers have served in the Peace Corps since the agency was established in 1961. Annually, approximately 8,000 Volunteer and trainees serve in more than 70 countries. They work in agriculture, education, environment, health and HIV/AIDS, community economic development, and youth in development.

"My daughter's Peace Corps experience guided her graduate school work and helped her land a great job addressing Latino health needs. I'm so proud that she lived overseas for two years and brought skills home to help improve the quality of life in our own community."

Libia McDonough, whose daughter served in Panama

"Our advice for parents whose children have a desire to go into the Peace Corps is to let them fulfill that desire. If the child is selected, the parents should feel extremely proud because it is an honor. The Peace Corps is life-changing. It will be the hardest job they've ever had and the one they will love the most."

Rebecca and Ronald Tubbs,
whose daughter served in Ukraine

This booklet is designed to help answer the most frequently asked questions from family and friends. It also provides information that can alleviate concerns and facilitate a supporting role in the Volunteer's success. The love and encouragement from folks "back home" is tremendously helpful for Volunteers as they embark on the experience of a lifetime.

For Parents, Family, and Friends

If a loved one is considering applying to the Peace Corps or currently serving in the Peace Corps, congratulations! Working as a Peace Corps Volunteer is an exceptional experience that furthers the cause of world peace and offers personal and professional growth. The selection process is competitive and it is an honor to be chosen to serve the U.S. while volunteering for a country that has asked for assistance.

The Peace Corps is committed to providing Volunteers with the support they need to successfully meet the challenges they face and to ensure a safe, healthy, and productive service. We hope the information here will help provide a sense of these challenges, the changes in attitude and lifestyle that may be required to adapt to a new environment, and the level of support that can be expected from the Peace Corps, local colleagues, and host communities.

Health and Safety

The health and safety of Volunteers is the Peace Corps' highest priority. One of the advantages to serving abroad with the Peace Corps is the safety net that comes from the agency being part of the federal government. Every country where Peace Corps serves has a medical staff and a safety and security coordinator assigned to provide health and safety services and train Volunteers. These staff members are supported by the Peace Corps Offices of Safety and Security, Victim Advocacy, Medical Services, and the Counseling and Outreach Unit in Washington, D.C.

There are inherent risks to living and traveling in countries where Peace Corps serves. However, the Peace Corps works to protect Volunteers with a thorough training program, medical and emotional support, and a comprehensive safety and security program, the highlights of which are outlined in the next few pages.

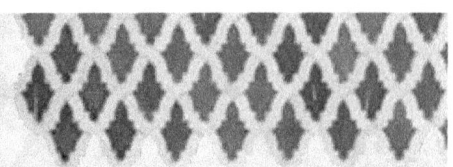

Safe and Productive Service

The Peace Corps takes an integrated approach to Volunteer training. Through language, cross-cultural, and health and safety instruction, the two- to three-month training is designed to raise trainees' awareness of their new environment, build their capacity to effectively handle the many challenges they may face, and provide tools they need to adopt a safe and appropriate lifestyle in the communities they will be serving. This includes testing for adequate communication skills in the local language before placing the Volunteers in their individual sites. During this period, most trainees live with a host family to fully immerse themselves in the new culture. The Peace Corps provides training on how to adapt personal choices and behavior to be respectful of the host country culture, which can have a direct impact on how Volunteers are viewed and treated by their new communities. The Peace Corps emphasizes professional behavior and cross cultural sensitivity to help integrate and be successful during service. The Peace Corps has global and country-specific policies and procedures in place to support safe and healthy Volunteers.

Volunteer Health

The comprehensive medical evaluation during the second stage of the application process ensures that a Volunteer is placed in a country that has adequate resources to meet the health care needs of the Volunteer. The Peace Corps staff includes at least one medical officer at each country's post. Nurses, nurse practitioners, physician assistants, and physicians can serve as Peace Corps medical officers. These medical providers include foreign-nationals and Americans. All are carefully evaluated, credentialed, and reviewed by the Peace Corps' Office of Medical Services Quality Improvement Unit at Peace Corps headquarters.

The medical staff in-country trains Volunteers on ways to stay healthy. Medical staff also provides Volunteers with basic medical skills and supplies, and primary care as needed. If a health problem occurs that cannot be treated locally, at the discretion of the Office of Medical Services, the Peace Corps, at its expense, will send the Volunteer to a regional facility or to the United States for treatment.

Prevention is an important part of each Volunteer's health care. The Peace Corps assumes the costs of necessary medical and dental expenses related to existing conditions at the time of entry into Peace Corps and to conditions that develop during Peace Corps service. Cosmetic and "lifestyle" medications and treatments are not paid by Peace Corps. Volunteers are eligible for benefits under the Federal Employee Compensation Act for most injuries or illnesses that occur during Peace Corps service.

Medical staff in-country and at headquarters are bound by medical confidentiality laws. A Volunteer's medical information may only be released to family or friends through the Volunteer's written consent. In a life-threatening situation, medical information may be shared with an emergency contact person previously identified by the Volunteer.

Other Medical Support Measures:

- *Up to 25 hours of health education, which integrates emotional health, as part of pre-service training.*

- *Mid-service and close-of-service physical and dental evaluations.*

- *Medical newsletters and training during service.*

- *Visits by the Peace Corps medical officer to the Volunteers' sites.*

- *In-country medical officer is on-call 24/7 for emergencies.*

Volunteer Safety Where They Live and Work

The Peace Corps assesses and approves the sites where Volunteers will live and work, ensuring these locations are appropriate and safe. Site selection is based on many criteria, such as site history; access to medical care and banking, postal, and other essential services; access to communication, transportation, and local markets; availability of adequate housing and living arrangements; and agreements with host country authorities and communities. Volunteers have work counterparts assigned to them in their communities. Volunteers often live with or near a host family. Peace Corps program managers and medical staff visit periodically to monitor issues related to Volunteers' site assignments. If a Volunteer's safety or well-being is at risk or compromised, the Peace Corps staff will help resolve the situation or move the Volunteer to another location.

Building Relationships is Key to Volunteer Safety

The unique arrangement of Peace Corps Volunteers living within the communities they serve integrates them through close interpersonal relationships with host-country nationals. This integration fosters an environment where Volunteers are considered to be part of the local community and, as such, are valued and protected as extended family members and respected colleagues. This arrangement has its advantages, but doesn't assure total safety – as crime can still occur. Peace Corps policies and training help mitigate Volunteer safety risks.

The Peace Corps Responds to Volunteers' Safety Concerns

Volunteers are trained and encouraged to report safety concerns or incidents to the appropriate Peace Corps staff member. The staff is prepared to provide medical, emotional, and administrative support as each case warrants, and Volunteer confidentiality is respected. Based on safety reports, the Peace Corps has identified risk factors and developed strategies to help Volunteers address them. Volunteers are urged to be aware of their environment and to adopt a safe lifestyle and exercise judgment in a manner that reduces their exposure to risks.

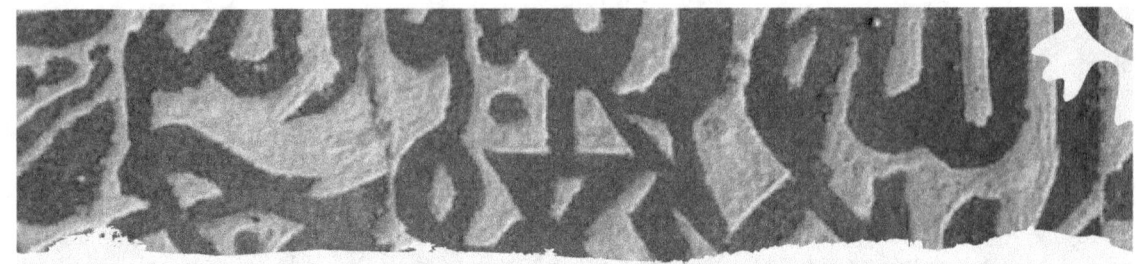

The Office of Victim Advocacy (OVA)

The OVA is a centralized resource to Volunteers who are victims of crime regarding the services they are entitled to receive. The office ensures Volunteer's voices are heard and considered in all decisions affecting their care and continued service in the Peace Corps.

Supporting Victims of Sexual Assault

The Peace Corps takes sexual assault very seriously and is committed to supporting Volunteers who have been victims of sexual assault. There are procedures in place in each country to respond quickly and compassionately to Volunteers. Teams of dedicated specialists from the medical, mental health, security, victim advocacy, and legal fields are also available at Peace Corps headquarters to help Volunteers, as

needed, with the recovery process. In addition to providing support to victims, the Peace Corps makes every effort to reduce the risk of sexual violence against Volunteers. Both staff and Volunteers participate in regular training on safety and security. This training covers a variety of topics related to the risk reduction of sexual assault. The Peace Corps has a reporting system to track and analyze safety and security incidents, and the data collected is used to augment and enhance Volunteer and staff training, both globally and at individual posts.

Emergency Communications and Planning

The Peace Corps addresses larger security concerns through country-specific Emergency Action Plans (EAPs) that are in place at each Peace Corps post and for which each Volunteer is trained. These plans, developed to address such events

as natural disasters or civil unrest, are tested and revised annually. A component of the EAP ensures that Volunteers can be contacted in case of an emergency and for important notices. The Peace Corps coordinates with the U.S. Embassy in each host country to share information, develop strategies, and coordinate communications. If a situation arises in a country that poses a potential threat to Volunteers, the Peace Corps will immediately assess the nature of the threat and respond in a manner that maximizes the Volunteers' safety and well-being. If a decision is made to evacuate Volunteers from a country, the Peace Corps will commit every resource at hand to safely move each Volunteer out of harm's way.

Most Volunteers live and work in communities at some distance from the Peace Corps office. As part of Peace Corps safety and security procedures, Volunteers are instructed to stay in touch with the Peace Corps office on a periodic basis. They are required to report their whereabouts when they travel from their communities, and are required to receive Peace Corps authorization if they intend to leave the country of assignment for any reason. Although some Volunteers consider notification of travel and keeping regular contact with the Peace Corps office restrictive, they are necessary to ensure Volunteers can be contacted in case of an emergency, including an emergency involving loved ones at home.

Additional Safety Information Resources

· *Comprehensive safety and security information is available at www.peacecorps.gov/safety*

Once Invited, Making an
Informed Choice to Serve

When an applicant is invited to serve in a particular country, general information, safety and security data, and specific information about potential challenges is provided in a Peace Corps *Welcome Book*. Challenges may include unwanted attention; harassment; health and safety risks; and cultural behaviors that an American might find uncomfortable or offensive. With this information, potential Volunteers can make informed decisions about whether Peace Corps service is appropriate for them and whether they are prepared to live in their host country, where their primary support system will be local community members. Once the Volunteers are in-country, Peace Corps staff will keep them informed of security issues and provide training and guidance for maintaining their safety and well-being. The Counseling and Outreach Unit at headquarters is available for emotional counseling for Volunteers experiencing adjustment challenges.

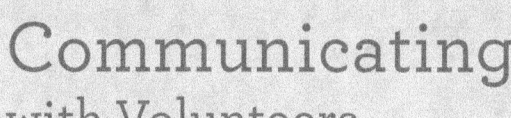

Communicating
with Volunteers

In our current culture, we have become accustomed to broad communication access through cell phone calls, text messaging, instant messaging, Internet chats, and email. While technology continues to improve even in the most remote places of the world, each country will have varying degrees of availability and reliability. Over 90 percent of Volunteers have cell phones and many Volunteers report having regular Internet access. In all countries, Volunteers can use computers when at the Peace Corps office. After adjusting to the particulars of a Volunteer's location, staying in touch with the Volunteer is possible.

Keep in mind that another country's postal system may not always be consistent or may take longer to distribute mail than in the U.S. It is not uncommon for correspondence to take several weeks for delivery and perhaps be delivered out of sequential order. For this reason, it is suggested that letters be numbered to keep track of correspondence. Also, consider carefully before sending items of great value. Packages, unfortunately, can get lost.

"Being parents of Peace Corps Volunteers, the most important part is to communicate as much as possible so you can understand what they are going through and what they are experiencing."

Petra and Fred Peng,
whose son served in the Philippines

Family Emergencies

The Peace Corps Counseling and Outreach Unit (COU) has a 24-hour duty officer available for family members needing to advise their Volunteer of a critical illness or death of a family member. **The 24-hour telephone number is 800-424-8580**; follow instructions for the headquarters office at extension 1470, or dial **202-692-1470**.

The COU can notify a Volunteer of an emergency, respond to family questions about a Volunteer's status, and supply an update about civil unrest or a natural disaster in the host country.

If a death occurs in a Volunteer's immediate family, the Peace Corps allows a leave period and pays for the Volunteer's travel home. Immediate family is defined as a parent, spouse, sibling, child, or grandchild related to the Volunteer by blood, marriage, or adoption. This includes step-relatives, (e.g., stepmother), but does not include in-laws, (e.g., mother-in-law), or grandparents.

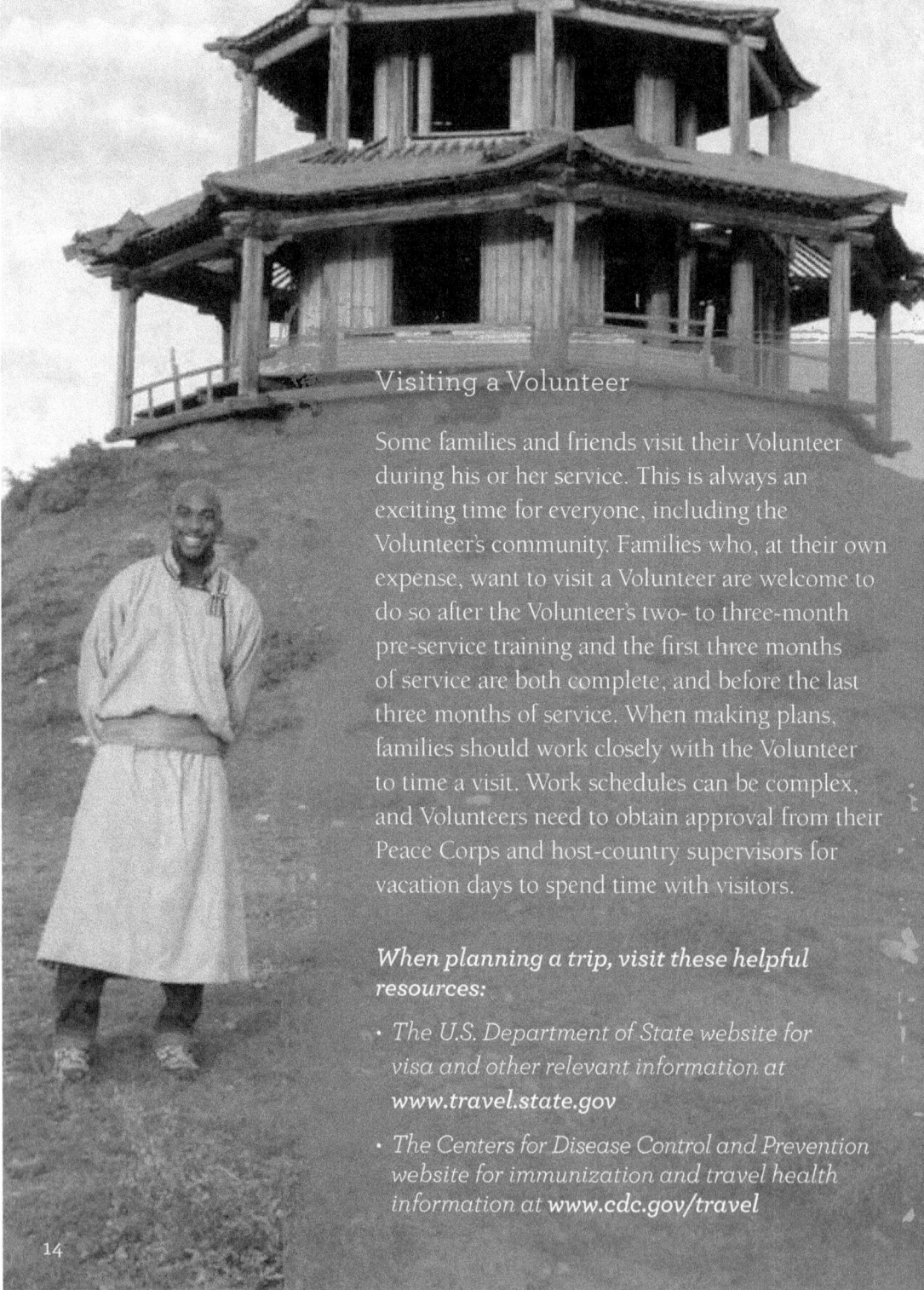

Visiting a Volunteer

Some families and friends visit their Volunteer during his or her service. This is always an exciting time for everyone, including the Volunteer's community. Families who, at their own expense, want to visit a Volunteer are welcome to do so after the Volunteer's two- to three-month pre-service training and the first three months of service are both complete, and before the last three months of service. When making plans, families should work closely with the Volunteer to time a visit. Work schedules can be complex, and Volunteers need to obtain approval from their Peace Corps and host-country supervisors for vacation days to spend time with visitors.

When planning a trip, visit these helpful resources:

· *The U.S. Department of State website for visa and other relevant information at **www.travel.state.gov***

· *The Centers for Disease Control and Prevention website for immunization and travel health information at **www.cdc.gov/travel***

Benefits of Serving

There are tangible benefits of Peace Corps service — financial, professional, and personal. Following is an overview of Peace Corps benefits.

- *Living allowance:* a monthly stipend to cover living and housing expenses
- *Vacation time:* earn two vacation days per month of service
- *Medical and dental coverage:* receive complete medical and dental care while serving
- *Student loan assistance:* some are eligible for deferment and some for partial cancellation
- *Graduate school opportunities:* unique programs both during and after Peace Corps service
- *Travel costs:* expenses for travel to and from the country of service are paid by the Peace Corps

- *Transition funds after service:* receive $7,425 (pre-tax after completing 27 months of service)
- *Marketable professional skills:* international experience with technical, language, and cross-cultural training
- *Advantages in federal employment:* creditable service and noncompetitive eligibility
- *Transition and job support services:* résumé assistance, career fairs, and online resources
- *Opportunities for short-term assignments:* returned Peace Corps Volunteers and Americans with 10+ years experience are eligible for Peace Corps Response
- *No Fee:* unlike other international volunteer programs, there is no fee to participate in the Peace Corps.

Learn more at
www.peacecorps.gov/benefits

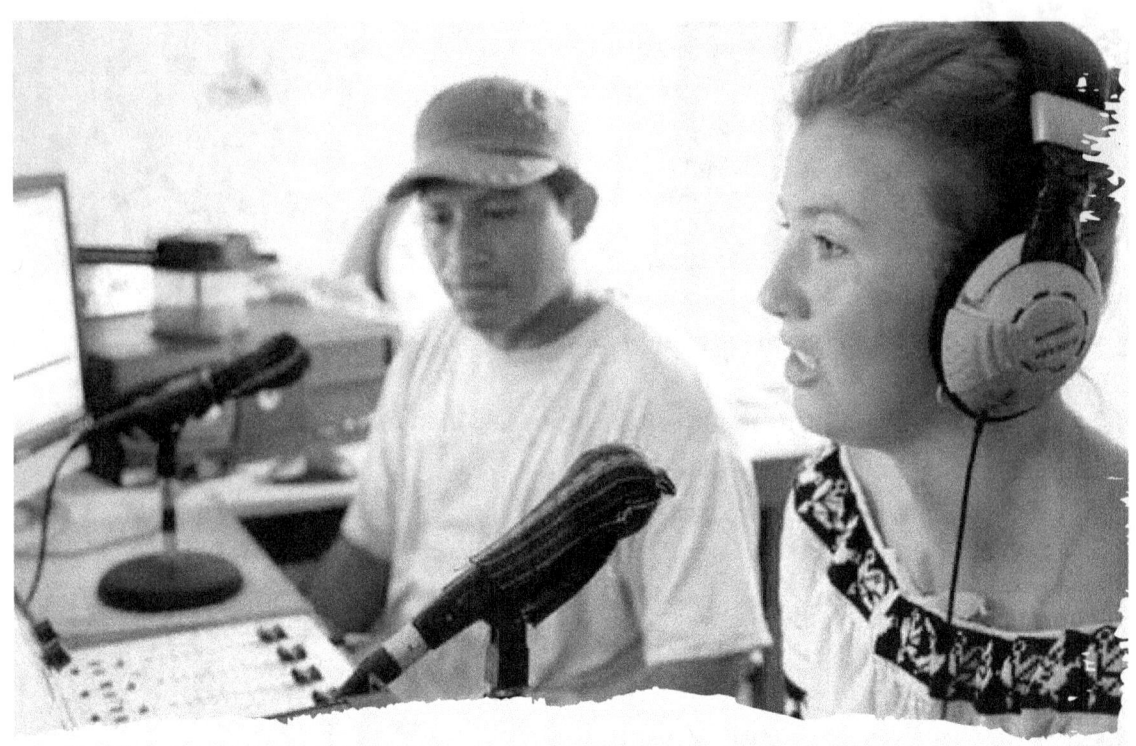

Career Builder

The Peace Corps is a life-defining leadership opportunity and a great way to launch a career in business, education, nonprofit organizations, and government. The Peace Corps also opens doors to graduate school through university partnership programs and provides experience that has recognition and value among admissions departments.

"Successfully completing Peace Corps under fairly challenging circumstances speaks a lot about character, fortitude, and the ability to take on difficult problems. When I see applicants with Peace Corps in their background, it is a real positive."

Frank Fountain, President,
The Chrysler Foundation
Returned Volunteer, India

"Peace Corps shaped our son in terms of turning what had been only thoughts into a career path. While he was serving in the area of public health, he got his commitment to medical school. Now he is a resident in emergency medicine at a hospital."

Phil Graitcer,
whose son served in Malawi

Graduate School Advantage

The Peace Corps offers two unique programs that combine Peace Corps service and graduate studies. Through partnerships with colleges and universities across the United States, Volunteers can earn academic credit for their Peace Corps service and/or may be awarded financial support.

Before and During Service

Volunteers can incorporate Peace Corps service as credit in a master's degree program in a variety of fields at over 80 academic institutions nationwide through **Master's International.**

Following Service

Returned Volunteers are offered financial assistance at more than 70 participating campuses in a variety of subject areas, combining graduate study with substantive, degree-related internships that help meet the needs of underserved U.S. communities through the **Paul D. Coverdell Fellows Program.**

*A list of participating schools and fields of study can be found at **www.peacecorps.gov/gradschool***

Skills for the Future

Fluency in foreign languages, international experience, and cross-cultural understanding are highly sought-after skills in today's global economy.

Receive Advantages in Federal Employment

Peace Corps service can qualify returned Volunteers to receive one year of noncompetitive eligibility for employment in the federal government. At an employing agency's discretion, if a Volunteer meets the minimum qualifications for a position, he or she may be hired without going through the standard competitive process. Those who are employed by the federal government after their Peace Corps service can receive credit toward retirement for their years of Volunteer service.

Returned Volunteers Make a Difference in the World

Returned Peace Corps Volunteers use the skills and experiences they gained overseas to help build careers in virtually every sector of our society. They are leaders, problem-solvers, and creative voices. They can be found in every walk of life, and many say their Peace Corps service had a profound impact on their careers.

View a list of some of the notable returned Peace Corps Volunteers at www.peacecorps.gov/notables

Transition and Job Placement Support

Before departing from their country of service, Volunteers are prepared for the transition back to the U.S. during a close-of-service conference. When Volunteers return to the U.S., the Peace Corps Office of Returned Volunteer Services provides them with transition assistance related to jobs and education.

Returned Volunteer Services

- *Publishes an online newsletter with job announcements, graduate school information, and career-related articles and advice.*

- *Sponsors career events throughout the year in Washington, D.C., and other cities around the U.S.*

- *Helps returned Volunteers translate their field experience for prospective employers and other professional contacts.*

Personal Development

The Peace Corps requires serious commitment and hard work. Volunteers leave the comforts of home and what is familiar, immerse themselves 24/7 in another culture, apply technical skills, and learn a new language that must be used every day – to shop for food, obtain transportation, develop friendships, and conduct work. The unique challenges of Peace Corps service make for a tremendous growth experience. Practical skills are gained and intangible benefits come with making a difference in people's lives and relying on oneself to respond to the needs of others.

The benefits of the Peace Corps don't end with overseas service and can be drawn upon throughout one's lifetime. As is often said, the Peace Corps isn't simply something great, it's the beginning of something great.

Helpful Resources
• Peace Corps website pages dedicated to Family and Friends
www.peacecorps.gov/family

• On the Homefront is a Peace Corps handbook
provided in hard copy 3-5 weeks prior to a Volunteer's
pre-departure orientation and is available online
www.peacecorps.gov/homefront

*"My daughter matured 10 years in her two years in the Peace Corps!
She made great friends, helped others, grew in her own self-confidence,
and is now in law school working to improve all our lives."*

*DeWitt Perkins,
whose daughter served in Senegal*

How Parents, Family,
and Friends Can Play a Part
in the Volunteer Experience

There are multiple ways to be involved with your Volunteer's experience.

- Support your Volunteer by staying connected through emails, phone calls, video chats, letters, and packages.

- Develop relationships with a returned Peace Corps Volunteer group (see www.rpcv.org) or join/create a support group founded by parents and family members. These groups are independent of the Peace Corps and are generally organized around a particular country or training group.

- Visit the Volunteer.

- Get involved in the Volunteer's projects through donations to the ***Peace Corps Partnership Program***. Volunteers often identify additional local needs in working with community leaders and may undertake secondary projects, such as building schools, latrines, or water wells, adding books to libraries, or providing technical trainings. Family, friends, or civic groups back home can support a Volunteer's project by giving even a modest sum through the Peace Corps Partnership Program.

*See **www.peacecorps.gov/contribute** for
current projects and information on giving*